DISCARDED

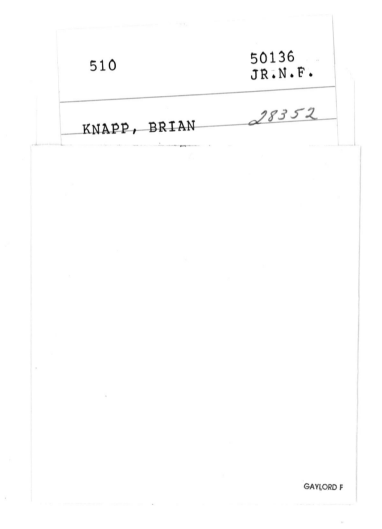

| 510 | 50136 |
| | JR.N.F. |

KNAPP, BRIAN   28352

GAYLORD F

Tables
and
Charts

Look out for these sections to help you learn more about each topic:

Remember…

This provides a summary of the key concept(s) on each two-page entry. Use it to revise what you have learned.

Word check

These are new and important words that help you understand the ideas presented on each two-page entry.

All of the word check entries in this book are shown in the glossary on page 45. The versions in the glossary are sometimes more extensive explanations.

Book link…

Although this book can be used on its own, other titles in the *Math Matters!* set may provide more information on certain topics. This section tells you which other titles to refer to.

Place value

To make it easy for you to see exactly what we are doing, you will find colored columns behind the numbers in all the examples on this and the following pages. This is what the colors mean:

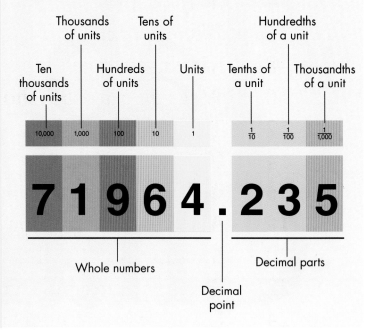

Ten thousands of units — 10,000
Thousands of units — 1,000
Hundreds of units — 100
Tens of units — 10
Units — 1
Tenths of a unit — $\frac{1}{10}$
Hundredths of a unit — $\frac{1}{100}$
Thousandths of a unit — $\frac{1}{1,000}$

71964.235

Whole numbers

Decimal point

Decimal parts

Series concept by *Brian Knapp and Duncan McCrae*
Text contributed by *Brian Knapp and Colin Bass*
Design and production by *Duncan McCrae*
Illustrations of characters by *Nicolas Debon*
Digital illustrations by *David Woodroffe*
Other illustrations by *Peter Bull Art Studio*
Editing by *Lorna Gilbert and Barbara Carragher*
Layout by *Duncan McCrae and Mark Palmer*
Reprographics by *Global Colour*
Printed and bound by *LEGO SpA, Italy*

First Published in the United States in 1999 by Grolier Educational, Sherman Turnpike, Danbury, CT 06816

Copyright © 1999
Atlantic Europe Publishing Company Limited

Library of Congress Cataloging-in-Publication Data
Math Matters!
    p. cm.
    Includes indexes.
    Contents: v.1.Numbers — v.2.Adding — v.3.Subtracting — v.4.Multiplying — v.5.Dividing — v.6.Decimals — v.7.Fractions – v.8.Shape — v.9.Size — v.10.Tables and Charts — v.11.Grids and Graphs — v.12.Chance and Average — v.13.Mental Arithmetic
ISBN 0–7172–9294–0 (set: alk. paper). — ISBN 0–7172–9295–9 (v.1: alk. paper). — ISBN 0–7172–9296–7 (v.2: alk. paper). — ISBN 0–7172–9297–5 (v.3: alk. paper). — ISBN 0–7172–9298–3 (v.4: alk. paper). — ISBN 0–7172–9299–1 (v.5: alk. paper). — ISBN 0–7172–9300–9 (v.6: alk. paper). — ISBN 0–7172–9301–7 (v.7: alk. paper). — ISBN 0–7172–9302–5 (v.8: alk. paper). — ISBN 0–7172–9303–3 (v.9: alk. paper). — ISBN 0–7172–9304–1 (v.10: alk. paper). — ISBN 0–7172–9305–X (v.11: alk. paper). — ISBN 0–7172–9306–8 (v.12: alk. paper). — ISBN 0–7172–9307–6 (v.13: alk. paper).

    1. Mathematics — Juvenile literature. [1. Mathematics.]
I. Grolier Educational Corporation.
QA40.5.M38   1998
510 — dc21   98–7404
                                                              CIP
                                                               AC

This book is manufactured from sustainable managed forests. For every tree cut down at least one more is planted.

Contents

Introduction

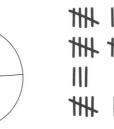

We do many things without realizing how we do them. One of them is looking at information.

For example, if the weather forecaster tells us that it will be **30**°C (**86**°F) tomorrow, we know that it will be a very hot day. We have done some pretty complicated number-crunching in our heads without even realizing it.

In a flash we have collected the information (heard it on the television), organized it (said to ourselves that this is temperature information), represented it (have thought, huh, this is a big number), and finally we have understood what it means (have thought that high temperatures means that it will be hot).

Country	Number of medals
United States	101
Germany	65
Russia	63
China	50
Australia	41
France	37
Italy	35
Korea	27
Cuba	25
Ukraine	23

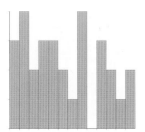

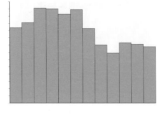

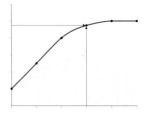

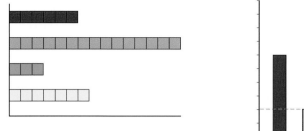

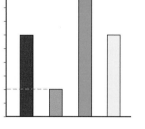

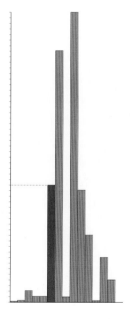

But it is not always that easy to understand the information available, and often we need the help of something to look at – tables and charts.

Any collection of numbers that is to be used as information in this way is called <u>data</u>.

Tables organize data by putting it into rows and columns. Charts use drawings to put data in a form that can be seen at a glance. But tables and charts are only useful if they are drawn using a few simple rules.

You will find that by following this book with its stage-by-stage approach, it will be easy to learn the ways of handling data and making useful tables and charts.

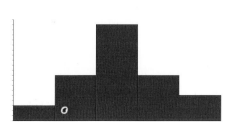

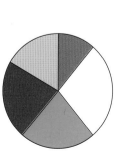

What is data?

Some things we do give us a lot of information that can be difficult to sort out. Number information is called data.

Here is a story about a girl who had to do a lot of counting and found a clever way of organizing her data.

The building set

Susie had a building set that held a lot of plastic bricks, windows, doors, and things that could be fitted together to make houses, castles, or all sorts of things.

It was a long time since she had used it. Now she took it out of the toy cupboard again because she wanted to make a house as part of a "My Town" project her class was doing at school.

When she looked inside the box, she found that she had **21** whole orange bricks, **155** purple ones, **62** blue ones, **40** green ones, and **178** red ones.

Susie wrote these numbers on a piece of paper. But then she had some half-size bricks and quite a lot of windows and doors, too. She also had **5** purple arches and some red roof tiles...

Word check
Data: Information from which you start to solve a problem. You might have collected it yourself or have been given it. The word comes from Latin meaning "things given."

Susie had been sorting different types of building pieces into piles and trying to count them, but she had so many piles! It was very confusing. She almost gave up.

So, she decided that it would be much easier if she sorted out the numbers, as well as the pieces, before she went any further.

Here are the building pieces that Susie organized and labeled. The numbers are called data. How they were sorted is shown on the next page.

Remember... Data is easier to handle when it is organized. The first task is to sort what you need from what you don't need.

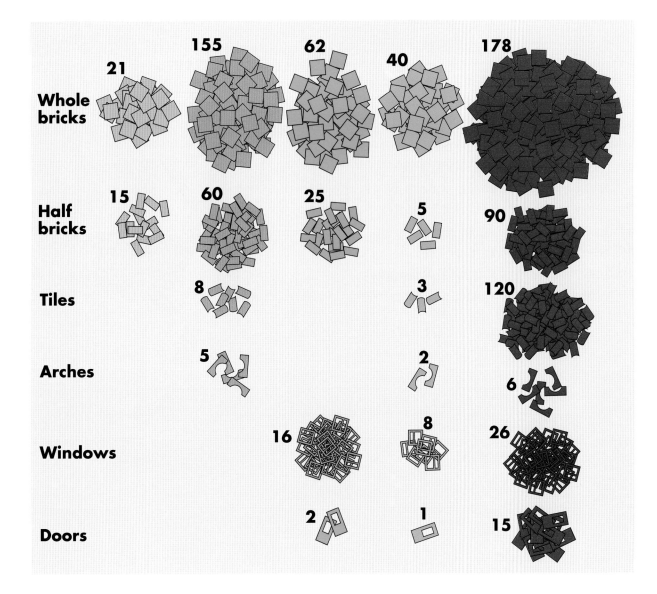

Making a table

A table is a good way to sort out data. The aim is to get a jumble of figures into an ordered pattern of rows and columns that can be easily understood. The ordered pattern is called a data table.

Table headings

Let's think about the colored building blocks shown on the previous page. They come in all sorts of shapes as well as colors.

If we write the names of the colors orange, purple, blue, green, and red across the page, leaving a space at the left-hand side, we are making headings for the columns that will form a table.

Down the left-hand side we can write the types of piece: whole bricks, half bricks, tiles, and so on. These make the headings for the rows of a table.

Since the table is large, drawing lines helps us keep all the numbers in their proper rows and columns.

Column headings

Building piece	Orange	Purple	Blue	Green	Red
Whole bricks					
Half bricks					
Tiles					
Arches					
Windows					
Doors					

Row headings

Placing the data

The numbers that go inside the table are the data.

To begin to fill in the table with data, we could start with the blue whole bricks. We write the number of blue whole bricks in the column underneath the word "Blue" and in the row beside the word "Whole bricks." In the set of data on page 6 you can see that there were 62. Look at the table below to see where the 62 has been placed.

Blue column

Whole bricks row

Building piece	Orange	Purple	Blue	Green	Red
Whole bricks	21	155	62	40	178
Half bricks	15	60	25	5	90
Tiles	0	8	0	3	120
Arches	0	5	0	2	6
Windows	0	0	16	8	26
Doors	0	0	2	1	15

When the data has all been filled in, you can see at a glance how many pieces of each color and type there were. For example, you can see that there were 8 purple tiles in the collection. Notice that we have put 0's in the places where there were no items.

By looking at the table, it is clear how many of each item were available. This is just what a table should do.

Remember... A table is an important way of sorting many categories in a way that makes them easy to understand.

Word Check

Column: Things placed one below the other. In a table the entries that are in a line that goes up and down the page.

Row: Things placed side by side. In a table the entries that are in any line across the page.

Table: An arrangement of rows and columns for sorting and storing data.

What does a table show?

A table is a much simpler way to find information than having to read a lot of sentences. On this page you will find two simple tables with just one column of numbers. This kind of table is also known as a list.

Arranging rows

There is no special order that you have to use to organize your rows and columns. In fact, you can often see answers more clearly if you juggle the rows and columns around.

Here is an example using medal winners from the 1996 Olympic Games. The top list has been organized so that the biggest number is at the top and the smallest number at the bottom. This list has been arranged by number.

The bottom table contains the same numbers, but this time the list has been sorted alphabetically by country, with A at the top and U at the bottom.

We have not changed the information but reorganized it. In the top table it is much easier to compare countries in terms of the medals they won. In the bottom table it is much easier to see the medals won by a particular country.

▼ Table of the Olympic Medals won in the 1996 games (first 10 countries listed) in medal order.

Country	Number of medals
United States	101
Germany	65
Russia	63
China	50
Australia	41
France	37
Italy	35
Korea	27
Cuba	25
Ukraine	23

▼ Table of the Olympic Medals won in the 1996 games (first 10 countries listed) in alphabetical order.

Country	Number of medals
Australia	41
China	50
Cuba	25
France	37
Germany	65
Italy	35
Korea	27
Russia	63
Ukraine	23
United States	101

Comparing numbers in a table

You can find out many interesting things from a table by comparing the numbers. On page 10 we have two tables showing some of the countries that won medals in the 1996 Olympic games.

Look at the tables number by number. Ask yourself these questions:

"Which is the biggest number?" Answer: 101. "Which is the smallest number?" Answer: 23.

Now look at any two numbers. Ask yourself, for example:

"How many more medals did the United States win than Cuba?" Answer: 101 − 25 = 76.

Do this for other countries. Now you can begin to see just how much information we can get from simple lists of numbers. The more you work at a table like this, the better you can understand it, and the more you find out.

Remember... A table allows you to make use of many combinations of numbers. This is why it is such a helpful way of organizing numbers.

Tallying

Tallying makes it easy to record data that you are collecting. It is a table because it accurately records numbers, but it is also a simple picture (or chart) of the data because the amount of space taken up increases with the number counted.

Tallying is also a way of counting using fives. The diagram on the right shows you what a tally of **5** looks like. Each tally of **5** is called a gate check.

If you stand by a roadside and count the number of cars, buses, bikes, and so on that pass, you might build up a tally. Or you could do it by counting how often selected words occur, as in the story about Ben described below.

▼ **A gate-check tally; four uprights and one sloping line make this look like a 5-bar farm gate.**

Ben was bored

It was a hot afternoon, and it was the school speech day. The principal had been droning on for ten minutes already when it occurred to Ben to take notes to keep himself awake. It did not do much for his "street-cred" until the others found out what he had been writing. All the children had been given programs of events on pieces of paper. Ben turned his over and wrote:

You see

I mean

Um

Finally

Then Ben kept a record of how many times the speaker used these words: "You see," "I mean," "Um," and "Finally."

Ben did it like this:

You see	||||
I mean	|||||
Um	||||||||||
Finally	||||||||

Ben could see that he might have a lot of counting to do. Because counting in 5's is easy, it would have been better to do it like this:

You see	||||
I mean	|||||
Um	||||| ||||| |
Finally	||||| |||

Later, Ben learned what is meant by a gate check. The fifth stroke crosses the first four like the bar of a gate and bundles all five together. This made the tally even easier to keep, as shown on the right.

You see	||||
I mean	ЖЖ
Um	ЖЖ ЖЖ |
Finally	ЖЖ |||

Remember… Counting data is much easier using gate-check groups of four upright and one slanting stroke.

Book link… Find out more about counting in the book *Numbers* in the *Math Matters!* set.

Word check

Chart: A diagram used to show data from tables. There are many kinds of charts, including bar charts and pie charts.

Gate check: Four upright tally marks with a fifth drawn across them, looking like a gate. It is used to speed up tallying.

Tallying: Making marks as a way of recording the total.

Pictograms

You can see that a tally score is a kind of mathematical picture, or chart. The more tally marks there are, the more space they take up. So just by standing back from a tally, you can see a pattern. However, by using symbols that represent the numbers collected, the chart can be made even easier to see. A chart using pictures is called a pictogram.

Traffic survey

Here are the results of a survey showing the different ways children in a class went to school.

Bus	卌 I	6
Car	卌 卌 卌	15
Bicycle	III	3
Walking	卌 II	7

To create a pictogram from the tally, first think of a suitable symbol to represent each tally line. In this case a symbol for people is used.

Now place the symbols side by side, one symbol per tally mark.

This gives us the pictogram shown on the right.

Bus	👤👤👤👤👤👤
Car	👤👤👤👤👤👤👤👤👤👤👤👤👤👤👤
Bicycle	👤👤👤
Walking	👤👤👤👤👤👤👤

Advertisement survey

Tania was surfing the web instead of doing the survey she had been assigned in class. Every page she looked at had an annoying advertisement on it. But then it occurred to her that she could survey the advertisements on the web for her coursework. This is what she found when she surfed 52 pages:

Subject	Tally	Total
Electronic goods	~~IIII~~ ~~IIII~~ IIII	14
Toys and games	~~IIII~~ ~~IIII~~ ~~IIII~~ ~~IIII~~ I	21
Making money	~~IIII~~ II	7
Vacations and travel	~~IIII~~ ~~IIII~~	10
Total		52

Then she tried representing each "hit" by a picture to make the results clear to see. This is the result:

Subject	Tally	Total
Electronic goods	▭▭▭▭▭▭▭▭▭▭▭▭▭▭	14
Toys and games	⊞⊞⊞⊞⊞⊞⊞⊞⊞⊞⊞⊞⊞⊞⊞⊞⊞⊞⊞⊞⊞	21
Making money	▤▤▤▤▤▤▤	7
Vacations and travel	✖✖✖✖✖✖✖✖✖✖	10
Total		52

Remember... Pictograms are fine for helping make results easier to see, but they can only be used when the number of items is small.

Word check

Symbol: A mark written on paper or something else to stand for a letter, a number, or an idea of any kind.

Bar charts

A bar chart uses bars instead of pictures. You can make bar charts from the numbers of a survey, or from tallies, or from a pictogram.

How to make bar charts

To make bar charts from pictograms or tallies, we make the length of each bar match the number of each category. This is called "drawing to scale." The bars can be drawn either across or up the page. If the bars are drawn up the page, the chart is often called a column chart.

As a first step we can draw the chart using squares, one square for each tally mark. The squares then "grow" out of an upright line, as you see in the sequence below.

Here we have made a bar chart from the school survey table on page 14.

Bus	卌 I
Car	卌 卌 卌
Bicycle	III
Walking	卌 II

Step 1: Set out the sorting categories (bus, car, etc.) on an upright line (called an axis), leaving gaps between each category. Set out a horizontal line (axis), and label it with what is being counted.

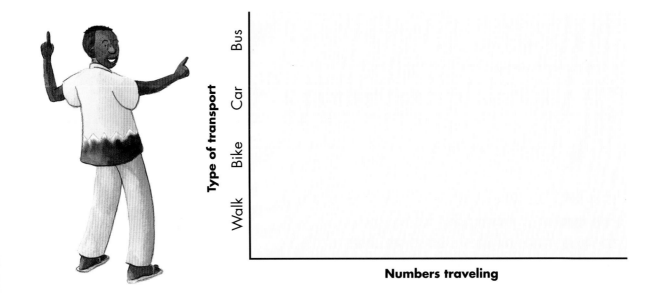

Numbers traveling

Step 2: Make the first bar by building up the bar out of squares for the bus category. There were **6** tally lines, so we have placed six squares side by side.

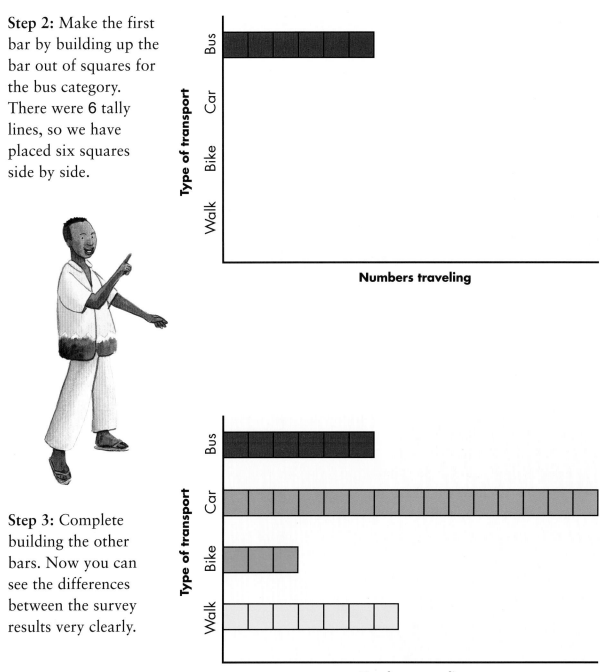

Step 3: Complete building the other bars. Now you can see the differences between the survey results very clearly.

Remember... When people speak of bar charts, they usually mean charts with the bars going across the page. Column charts have bars going up the page.

Note: You will find out how to add scales to all of these charts on page 21.

Add numbers to your charts

Adding numbers to charts means that they can be more easily read by other people. Here we will make up a column chart, which is a bar chart in which the information appears in rising columns. We will also add some numbers to show how long each column is.

For a column chart the sorting categories go across the page from left to right.

First make sure you see that the column and tally charts are really the same. Start with the tally chart on its side, with the tallies pointing up. This will give you an idea of what the final chart will look like, as you can see on the right. Notice the tally results on this page are different from those on page 16 to give you more charts to compare.

Step 1: Begin to draw the chart as on page 16. In this case the sorting categories go across the page on the horizontal axis. The squares will "grow" up from the bottom line.

What is being counted goes on the upright line, or vertical axis.

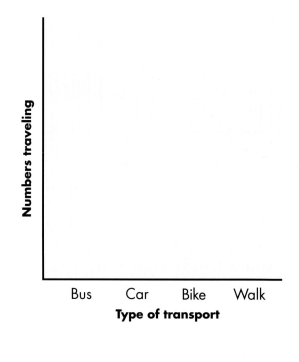

Step 2: In exactly the same way as we did on page 17, we build up the first column out of squares for the bus category.

In this case there were also **6** tally lines, so we have placed six squares on top of each other.

Step 3: Complete building the other columns to make the finished column chart.

Writing numbers on top of each column tells us how long it is without having to count the squares. It is best to add numbers to the ends of all forms of bar chart.

Remember... In charts like these that use separate categories, make sure the columns do not touch each other.

Making use of scales

The charts on the previous pages were made by building squares. Because we used squares, we could count up the number of squares to find out how big each bar or column was. But this can be time-consuming, which is the reason why we added numbers to the bars and columns on page 19.

Step 1: Start with the column chart shown on the bottom of page 19. The numbers at the top of each column tell us quickly how many squares it contains.

Because we have numbers on each column, we don't need the squares, so we can take away the dividing lines to show the number counted as a single column.

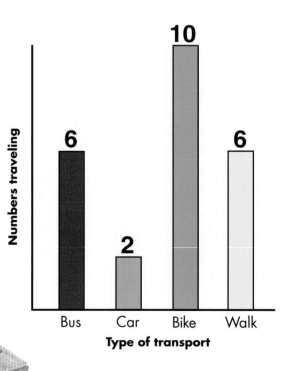

Step 2: Now we are going to add a scale. A scale is a line marked out evenly to show value.

The scale line shown here has been drawn up the side of the chart.

The numbers have been spaced evenly on the line.

You can see that the tops of the columns match numbers on the scale. The shortest column was made of **2** squares. The brown dotted line shows that the top of the column exactly matches the **2** on the scale, so we can still find out how much each column is worth without cluttering the chart with numbers.

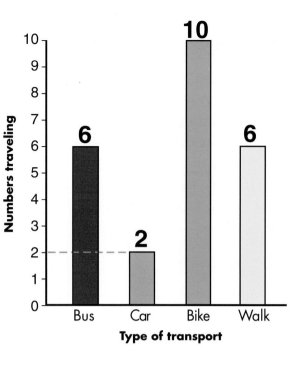

This is the same chart turned on its side to make it into a bar chart. Notice that the scale is now shown across the page, but otherwise it is marked up in exactly the same way as the column chart at the top of the page.

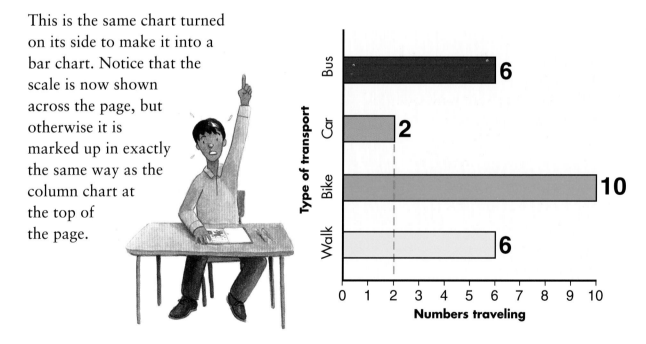

Remember... When the scale shows numbers that have been <u>counted</u>, the ends of the columns or bars are exactly level with those numbers on the scale.

Word check
Scale: A set of marks on a line used for measuring.

Rules for drawing charts

Charts are built up from information. The purpose of a chart is to allow us to see information or data more clearly.

But at the same time, we must not lose information, nor must we make a chart that gives a misleading impression. So all charts have to be drawn following some rules.

Rule 1: If the chart contains collections of different types of information, such as the T-shirt colors shown on this page, then the bars or columns must all be the same width, and they must be spaced apart. They <u>must</u> <u>not</u> touch or overlap.

However, when the chart contains things that change continuously – such as the rainfall charts on page 23 – the bars <u>should</u> touch, since, for example, February follows January without a break.

Rule 2: The number scale must have numbers next to the ticks, not in the spaces between them. It is usually easier to read scales based on multiples of 1, 2, and 5 (e.g., 3 squares to represent 10 car journeys would be hard to interpret).

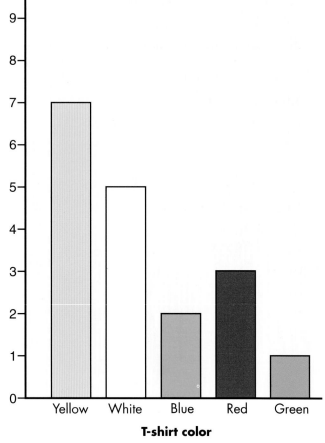

Because the headings are short, this chart has columns wide enough for the headings to be written sideways. This makes the labeling easy to read.

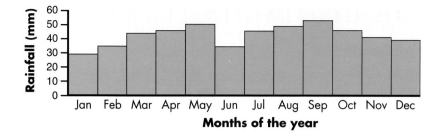

◄ **This chart is too squashed. It is hard to find out the value of each bar.**

▼ **This chart is too tall and thin. It is hard to compare the smallest and largest units**

Rule 3: Make the scale suitable for the information you are presenting.

The two charts on this page show you what can go wrong. They both contain the same data, but in the top chart the scale for rainfall is too squashed, while in the one below it is too drawn out. A well-balanced rainfall chart, using different data, is on page 34.

Rule 4: Always begin your number scale with zero if at all possible.

Rule 5: It is often helpful for the columns to be wide enough for their headings. However, if the headings are too long, they can sometimes be shortened (for example, August to "Aug," or simply "A") or be written sideways below their columns (see the chart on page 29).

Remember... A good chart takes time to draw, but this is time well spent since it makes the information clearer to see.

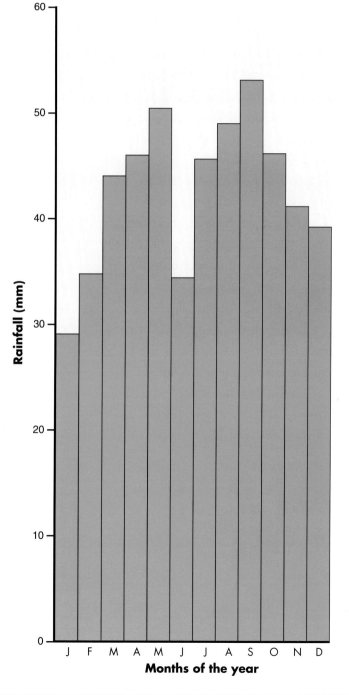

Charts with numbers in order

In the charts we have drawn so far, the categories were mainly things like "bus" and "bike" or "T-shirt color." There is no obvious order in which to arrange them. But when we drew the rainfall chart, you could see that we had to put the columns in order of the months if the chart was to make sense. In general, when you have numbered categories, it is usual to arrange them in numerical order: **1, 2, 3, 4, 5, 6...** The example below shows you when numbered categories should be placed in order.

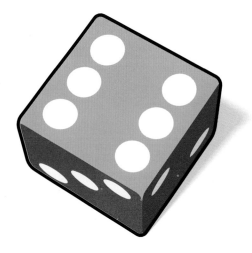

Playing with dice

Charlie's class was doing a project on dice. In the long run, when you throw dice, each of the marked faces is supposed to come out on top the same number of times. But does it? That is what Charlie's class was trying to find out.

Charlie threw his die **100** times and tallied the scores. On the right is a table of Charlie's results.

Charlie did not score each number equally often. He drew a column chart of his results.

▼ Table of number of times each marked face was thrown by Charlie

Number	Tally	Number of times
1	卌 卌	10
2	卌 卌 卌 卌 I	21
3	卌 卌 卌 I	16
4	卌 卌 卌 IIII	19
5	卌 卌 IIII	14
6	卌 卌 卌 卌	20

▼ Chart of number of times each marked face was thrown by Charlie

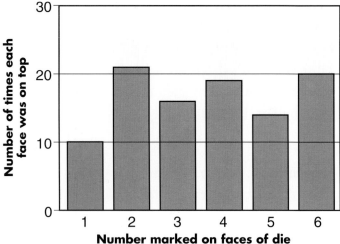

The teacher collected the results from everybody in the class, and they made another table and column chart. Since there were **30** students in the class, they had **3,000** results altogether.

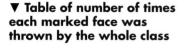

▼ Table of number of times each marked face was thrown by the whole class

Score	Number
1	495
2	515
3	491
4	509
5	496
6	494

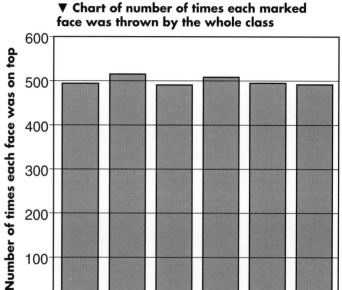

▼ Chart of number of times each marked face was thrown by the whole class

They arranged the number columns in order, and they started their scale at zero. Notice that they had to change the upright scale because there were more results. Using all of these results, it did seem that in the long run, all six faces might land upward an equal number of times.

Remember... In this chart the bottom line is marked **1, 2, 3, 4, 5, 6**. These are separated numbers because you cannot possibly score something between any of them (say between **1** and **2**). When numbered categories have separated numbers, the columns do not touch each other. They are drawn separately. But they are kept in numerical order.

Word check
Separated numbers: Numbers that increase in steps. For example, shoe sizes increase through 6, 6½, 7, 7½. You cannot get sizes between these numbers.

Grouping data before making a chart

In many cases the way that we gather data gives us natural categories, or groups. For example, we group rainfall into months. But sometimes the data appears to be too much to handle on a chart unless we do something with it first. Here is an example.

Telephone trouble

A bank employs people to answer telephone enquiries from customers. The directors of the bank decided to do a survey to find out more about the pattern of the enquiries.

▼ **Table of number of calls taken and the days when that happened**

Number of calls taken on a day = x
Number of days when that happened = y

Grouping

The first results were set out in a table as shown on the right.

A chart of this data is shown at the top of page 27.

This first table shows the results as they were presented to the directors by the survey company. They presented a list, showing the number of days each number of calls was made.

x	y	x	y	x	y	x	y	x	y
50	0	60	2	70	1	80	1	90	0
51	1	61	1	71	2	81	1	91	1
52	0	62	1	72	3	82	2	92	0
53	0	63	0	73	1	83	2	93	0
54	1	64	1	74	2	84	1	94	1
55	0	65	1	75	2	85	0	95	1
56	0	66	0	76	2	86	1	96	1
57	1	67	1	77	1	87	1	97	1
58	0	68	1	78	2	88	0	98	0
59	0	69	1	79	3	89	0	99	0

The directors found the first results confusing, so they grouped the data to make a second table.

A chart of the grouped data is also shown on page 27.

This shows that between 80 and 89 calls were taken on 9 days of the survey.

▼ **Table of grouped data showing number of calls taken and the days when that happened**

Number of calls taken on a day	Number of days when that happened
50–59	3
60–69	9
70–79	19
80–89	9
90–99	5

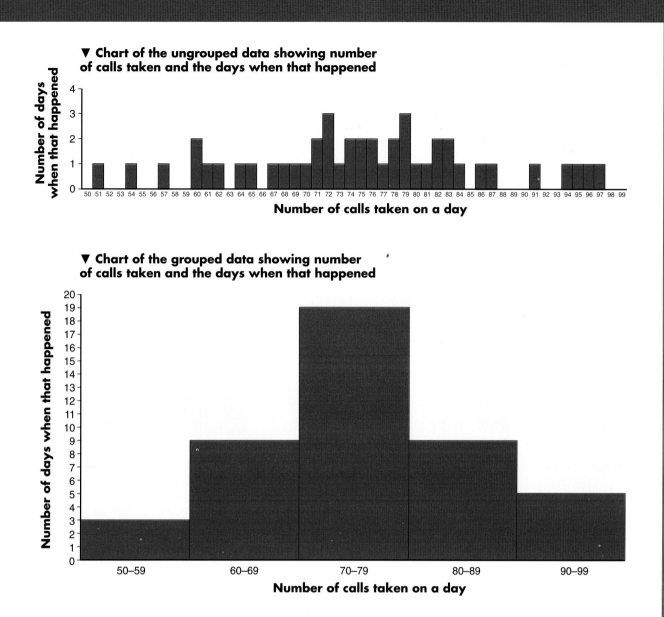

▼ Chart of the ungrouped data showing number of calls taken and the days when that happened

Number of days when that happened

Number of calls taken on a day

▼ Chart of the grouped data showing number of calls taken and the days when that happened

Number of days when that happened

Number of calls taken on a day

The benefits of grouping

The point about grouping is that it can turn data that makes no sense at all into something that is usable.

Unfortunately, there are no rigid rules to help you know what kind of groups to make. Knowing how to group data is a matter of experience. But this example shows you what you are aiming for.

For instance, by grouping into tens, it is now easy to see that the most common number of callers each day is between 70 and 79, so the directors can plan to use enough telephone operators to cope with this number of enquiries.

Remember… Grouping data often makes the information simpler to understand.

Time charts

Time charts are an important type of chart. The rainfall chart on page 23 is a time chart. Here is another typical case when a time chart is needed.

Wagons ho!

In a lesson about the people who traveled long distances in the past, a class was learning about pioneering journeys.

One of the most famous of these pioneering journeys was made by those who walked halfway across the North American continent to begin a new life in the West. It became known as the Oregon Trail.

The records of the numbers of people who traveled west each year are shown in the table below.

▼ Table of the number of people who walked along the Oregon Trail

Year	Number traveling
1844	120
1845	300
1846	2,000
1847	1,000
1848	1,000
1849	21,000
1850	45,000
1851	1,000
1856	8,000
1852	52,000
1853	20,000
1854	12,000
1855	300
1856	8,000
1857	4,000
1858	0

Charting the use of the trail

The chart is drawn with time shown across the page and traveler numbers shown up the page.

Step 1: Decide on the scale. Notice that the largest numbers (**52,000**) traveled in **1852**. The scale has to be long enough for **52,000**. But our smallest number is **0**, so the scale begins at zero.

The scale increases by **1,000** for each tick. To make it easy to read, the last three 0's have been taken off each number, and the label for the scale has been written to explain that each number is "thousands."

Step 2: Begin each column. The columns on this chart will touch each other because they represent years. The name of the year is written under each column, and the axis labeled "Year."

Step 3: Now each column is completed. This is how the **1849** column is drawn:

Starting on the number scale at **21,000**, a line is ruled across where the column of year **1849** is to be drawn. The column lines are then drawn up from the year line to meet it.

All the other columns are drawn in the same way.

Remember... In this chart the time on the bottom line increases by years. We draw the columns touching because one year immediately follows another.

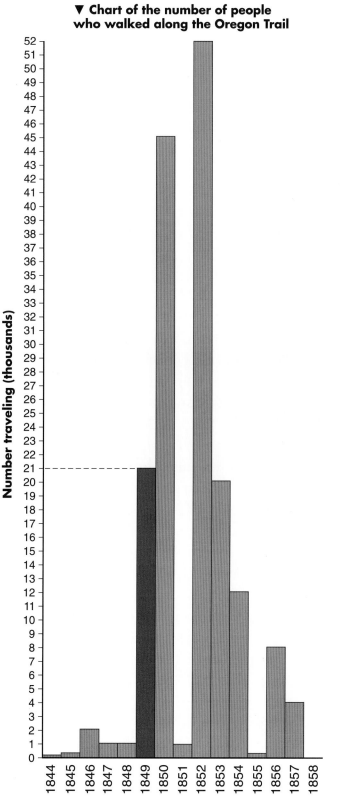

▼ **Chart of the number of people who walked along the Oregon Trail**

29

More time charts

As we have seen earlier in this book, some things that you want to investigate change in an even way. Your age is like this. It does not <u>really</u> increase in stages, but it <u>seems</u> to if you only count the years and jump from being eight to being nine on your birthday. This is how to chart age information.

The ages in a class

Liz's class had to gather some data for drawing charts. Liz suggested that they should find out the ages of all the children in their class. After the class had talked about it, they decided to chart years and months, but not the days.

The results they found for the 30 students in their class are shown in the table on the right and in the chart on page 31. In this case it is better not to have spaces between the columns on the chart but to make them touch because one month follows after another.

The numbers along the bottom line are now written below the ticks to show the point when a student's age changes. The three students shown in the first column are between 8 years 7 months and 8 years 8 months old.

Notice that we have chosen a scale for the upright axis that will make the difference in column heights easy to see.

▼ Table of the age of students in the class

Age	Number
8 years 7 months	3
8 years 8 months	4
8 years 9 months	2
8 years 10 months	3
8 years 11 months	3
9 years 0 months	2
9 years 1 months	1
9 years 2 months	4
9 years 3 months	0
9 years 4 months	3
9 years 5 months	2
9 years 6 months	1
9 years 7 months	2

▼ Chart of the ages of students in the class

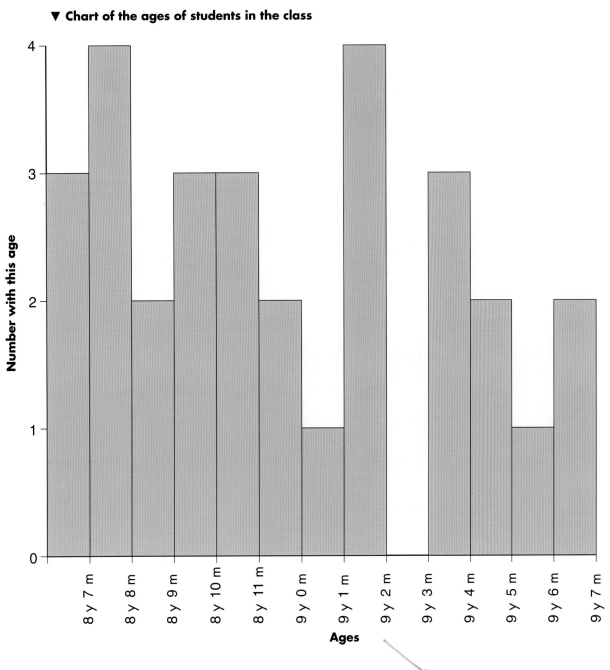

Number with this age (y-axis: 0, 1, 2, 3, 4)

Ages (x-axis): 8 y 7 m, 8 y 8 m, 8 y 9 m, 8 y 10 m, 8 y 11 m, 9 y 0 m, 9 y 1 m, 9 y 2 m, 9 y 3 m, 9 y 4 m, 9 y 5 m, 9 y 6 m, 9 y 7 m

Remember... Since this is a time chart, the columns touch.

Word check
Continuous scale: A number scale that increases smoothly.

A chart showing spread

Many charts show the spread of results around an average. This is what this type of chart looks like and what you can learn from it.

Lourdes and the beanstalks

Lourdes's class was doing a science experiment. They grew beans in flower pots on the window sill for some time, and then, during a science lesson, they measured how high they were.

After the class had discussed the problems of measuring, they decided to record the height of the stem to the nearest centimeter without straightening it.

The table on the right and the chart on page **33** show the results of **135** beans that the students in Lourdes's class recorded.

The columns are not separated because heights vary smoothly.

The number scale

When you measure to the nearest centimeter, any height that is between, say, **30.5** cm and **31.5** cm will be recorded as **31** cm. Alternatively, you could label each column as, for example, 30.5–31.5.

Getting the best presentation

When you draw a chart, you are the one who decides how to group the data. You can do this in different ways, and sometimes it makes the chart a great deal more helpful.

▼ Table of the height of beanstalks in the experiment

Height (cm)	Number of beanplants
25	1
26	0
27	4
28	7
29	11
30	9
31	24
32	39
33	23
34	8
35	6
36	2
37	1

In this case the class could have decided to group the heights of the stems to the nearest **2** cm centered on **26, 28, 30,** and so on, or to the nearest **2** cm centered on **25, 27, 29, 31.** This would have made quite a difference. You may like to try this to see for yourself.

If you have too many columns, the pattern gets confusing. But if you do not have enough columns, the pattern gets hidden. Using between **7** and **15** columns is often best.

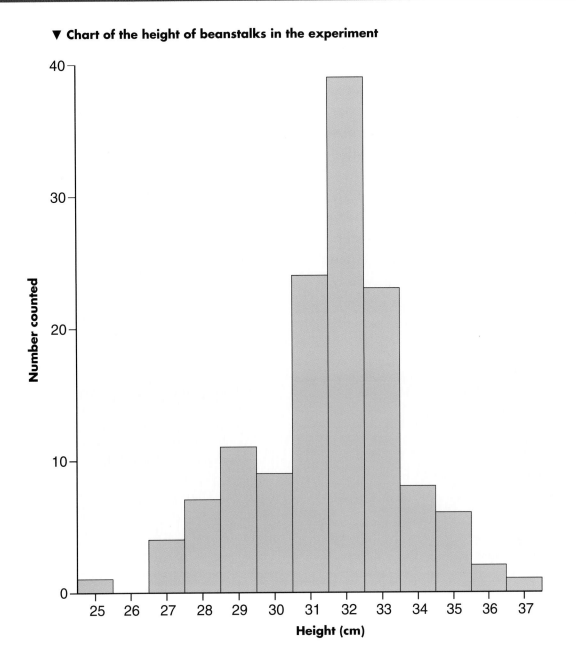

▼ **Chart of the height of beanstalks in the experiment**

Remember... Take care over grouping your data to get the best presentation.

Book link... This type of chart enables you to see the most common value, the mode (tallest column), and the range of the data very clearly. To find out more about averages, spread, and range, see the book *Chance and Average* in the *Math Matters!* set.

Word check

Average: A number that gives you, in different ways, a single typical value for the data you have. Most people use the word average when they are actually talking about the mean.

Mode: One form of average. The number or the group of numbers that occurs most often in the data.

Range: The difference between the largest and the smallest records in data. It tells you how widely data are spread.

Spread: A number that tells you how variable data are. It is often measured using the range.

Rainfall charts

In most charts on the previous pages the height of a column or the width of a bar has matched a tick on the scale. But in some cases this will not be so, as the rainfall data on this page shows.

We use the same kind of upright scale, with the same kind of numbering, and with the numbers right alongside the ticks as before. The difference is that the column heights no longer need to line up exactly with a number on the scale, but instead, their heights match the rain that actually fell.

▼ Chart of the amount of rainfall in a year

By reading off the scale, we can find out that in January 104 mm of rain fell.

Note: In this rainfall chart the bottom line shows continuous time grouped into months. So the columns of the chart should touch each other.

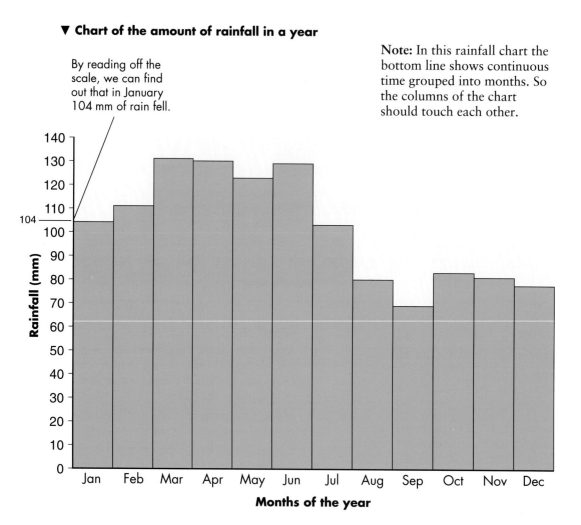

Finding the total

To find the total yearly rainfall from a chart, you need to know how to read the columns.

Look at the top of the column on the left of this chart. This gives the total rain that fell in January. It is **104** mm.

To find the rainfall total for the whole year, you need to write down each of the monthly numbers in a column and add them. In this case the total was **1,222** mm.

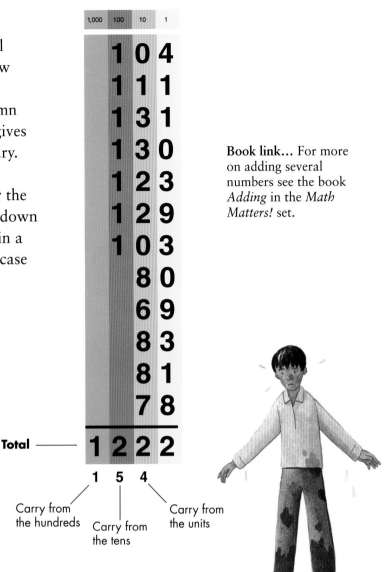

1,000	100	10	1
1	0	4	
1	1	1	
1	3	1	
1	3	0	
1	2	3	
1	2	9	
1	0	3	
	8	0	
	6	9	
	8	3	
	8	1	
	7	8	

Total — **1 2 2 2**

1   5   4

Carry from the hundreds

Carry from the tens

Carry from the units

Book link... For more on adding several numbers see the book *Adding* in the *Math Matters!* set.

Remember... You can group categories together to find totals for different reasons. For example, with the rainfall chart on page 34 you don't have to add all of the monthly column heights together to find a total for the year. Instead, you could group months to find the totals for spring, summer, autumn, and winter.

Word check

Digit: The numerals 1, 2, 3, 4, 5, 6, 7, 8, 9, or 0. Several may be used to stand for a larger number. They are called digits to make it clear that they are only part of a complete number.

Carrying: In adding, when the working column total is bigger than 10, this is the method of adding the left digit at the bottom of the column on the left.

Line graphs

Sometimes we want a picture of what is happening moment by moment. In these cases we simply plot the data points and join the plotted points with a smooth curve, as you can see in this example of temperature changes.

Boiling point experiment

Kah Tin was doing an experiment to find out how a liquid changed temperature as it was heated.

He placed a thermometer in the flask containing the liquid and stood this on a heating plate. Every 60 seconds he recorded the temperature as shown by the thermometer.

Here are the results:

▼ Table of data showing the temperature of water during the experiment.

Time from start of experiment (sec)	Temperature (°C)
0	20
60	50
120	80
180	95
240	100
300	100

Although the temperature was only measured every 60 seconds, the temperature was rising all the time.

Plotting a line graph

To plot these data as a line graph, put time on the bottom line (the x-axis) and temperature on the upright line (the y-axis) as shown at the top of page 37. In this case the time has been marked off in 60-second intervals to match when the recordings were made.

The upright scale has been marked off in 20°C intervals.

To plot a point, say, time = 180 seconds, temperature = 95°C, run up from the 180 mark on the time scale and across from the 95 position on the temperature scale. Where they meet, mark a point. Notice that 95 is not marked on the scale, so you will have to estimate where 95 should be.

Now join the plotted points with a smooth curve.

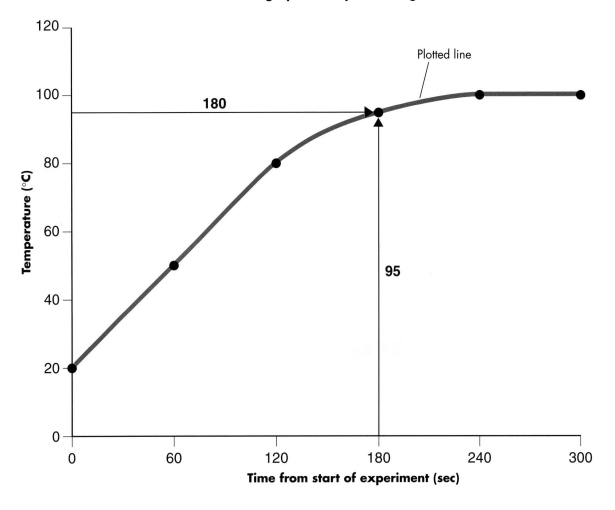

▼ A line graph of temperature against time

Plotted line

Temperature (°C)

Time from start of experiment (sec)

180

95

Reading from the graph

To find the time it took to reach any temperature, you run across from the temperature scale, then down to the time line. Read the number from the time line.

Remember... Line graphs are used for continuously changing information, such as the results of science experiments.

Word check

Graph: A diagram with two axes on which points are plotted and then joined by lines.

Book link... Find out more about line graphs in the book *Grids and Graphs* in the *Math Matters!* set.

Line charts

Line charts and line graphs (page 36) are two ways of showing how data vary by drawing a line. These two kinds of illustration may look similar, but in fact they are not.

The chart shown on page 39 is <u>not</u> a line graph. It is a line chart. A line chart is really a column chart with the top of the column marked by a dot and the columns removed. It is not a graph at all.

Students at school

The table to the right shows the total number of students at a school year by year. To draw a line chart of the data, you make a dot above each year at the height where the top of the column would have been. Then you join the points up with <u>straight</u> lines.

The only numbers you can choose are the whole numbers that are marked.

The numbers on the bottom scale are separated, and the numbers on the top line are counted. The chart is really a column chart with separated columns.

Column charts take a long time to draw. To save time, many people use a line chart like the one on this page, instead.

Year	Roll
1990	365
1991	380
1992	390
1993	385
1994	410
1995	397
1996	415
1997	370
1998	378
1999	420

◄ Table of the total number of students at a school year by year.

▼ The chart below has been prepared with a scale starting at 0. Notice how it makes each year look similar because the results are squashed up. It might be used to suggest that the school roll was much the same each year.

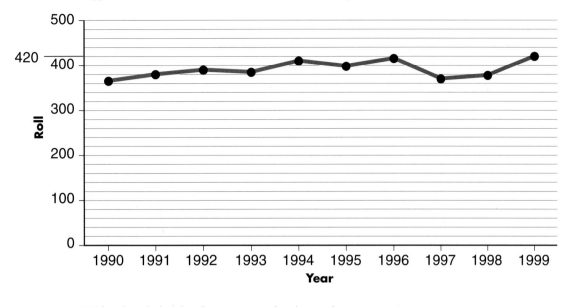

▼ The chart below has been prepared with a scale starting at 340. Notice how it makes the differences between years seem very large. It might be used to suggest that the school roll changed dramatically from year to year.

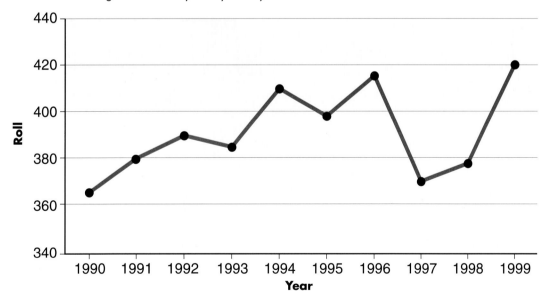

Remember... As long as you understand the difference between a line chart and a line graph, you can use line charts. But a column chart is always a more accurate way to show the data.

Word check

Chart: A diagram used to show data from tables. There are many kinds of charts, including bar charts and pie charts.

Graph: A diagram with two axes on which points are plotted and then joined by lines.

Pie charts using percentages

Pie charts are circular diagrams that are divided up into sectors like portions of a pie.

When to use a pie chart

The table on the right shows the results of a survey of how students get to school.

In this case we are interested in knowing what proportion of the students come by car. This would, for example, allow us to compare schools that have very different numbers of students.

Percentages are a good way of comparing proportion and can be used to make up a pie chart as shown here, using a pie-chart measurer.

▼ Table of the collected data from a survey on how people get to school.

Transport	Number
Bus	48
Bike	20
Car	94
Walk	38
Total	200

Drawing a pie chart with a pie-chart measurer

First turn the results from the survey into percentages. Divide the number in each category by the total, and multiply by 100. For example, the percentage of students arriving by bus is:

$$\frac{48}{200} \times 100 = 24\%$$

▼ Table of data from the survey turned into percentages.

Transport	Percent (%)
Bus	24
Bike	10
Car	47
Walk	19
Total	100

Now we can make up the pie chart.

First, draw a circle with a compass. Then, using a ruler, draw a radius line from the center to the boundary of the circle at the 12 o'clock position. This is the first edge of the first sector.

Then we use a pie-chart measurer. Place the zero line of the pie-chart measurer on this radius line. Use a pencil to mark off **24%**. Draw another radius line to this point to make the sector for the students who traveled by bus.

Place the zero line of the pie-chart measurer on one edge of the bus sector, and use a pencil to mark off a further **10%** to make the sector for the students who traveled by bike.

Continue like this until you have drawn all the slices. If you have worked accurately, you will have got back exactly to where you started, at **100%**.

Your final result should look like the pie chart on the right.

Remember... Pie charts can show percentages of the total in each category. They do not show you the total amount in each category.

The bigger the sector, the bigger the percentage of the total, and therefore the bigger the proportion.

Book link... Find out more about percentages in the book *Fractions* in the *Math Matters!* set. To find out more about angles, see the book *Size* in the *Math Matters!* set.

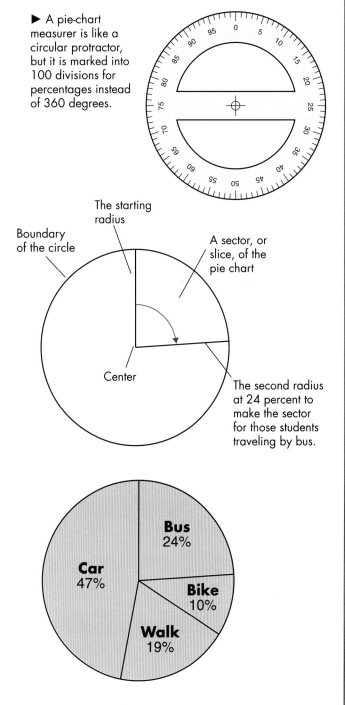

▶ A pie-chart measurer is like a circular protractor, but it is marked into 100 divisions for percentages instead of 360 degrees.

The starting radius

Boundary of the circle

A sector, or slice, of the pie chart

Center

The second radius at 24 percent to make the sector for those students traveling by bus.

Bus 24%

Bike 10%

Walk 19%

Car 47%

Word check

Fraction: A special form of division using a numerator and denominator. The line between the two is called a dividing line.

Percent: A number followed by the % symbol means the number is divided by 100. It is a way of writing a fraction.

Proportion: A comparative share of something.

Sector: A piece of a circle, like a piece of a pie.

Pie charts using degrees

Pie charts can also be drawn using degrees. Each category is converted into a proportion of a complete, **360** degree, turn.

The table on the right shows the data a class had collected about the colors of their shoes. Because there were different numbers of girls and boys in the class, we cannot immediately compare the numbers wearing each color of shoe. What we need to do first is to turn the numbers into degrees. Once made into degrees, the results can then be drawn as a pie chart.

▼ **Table of colors of students' shoes**

Shoe color	Girls	Boys
Brown	2	7
White	5	5
Blue	4	2
Red	4	0
Tan	3	1
Total	18	15

Drawing pie charts with a protractor

Work out how many degrees should represent each of the results for girls. There are **360** degrees in the whole turn of a circle. Divide **360** by the total number of girls, which is **18**:

360 ÷ 18 = 20

So each (1) girl in the table is represented by 20 degrees.

Now multiply the number of girls with each shoe color by **20** degrees. This is the size of the pie slice, or sector, for that category in degrees.

For example, the **2** girls with brown shoes are represented by **40** degrees in a turn:

2 × 20 = 40

The calculations for all the categories are shown in the table at the top of page 43.

▼ Table of colors of students' shoes shown as degrees

Shoe color	Girls' angles (degrees)	Boys' angles (degrees)
Brown	2 × 20 = 40	7 × 24 = 168
White	5 × 20 = 100	5 × 24 = 120
Blue	4 × 20 = 80	2 × 24 = 48
Red	4 × 20 = 80	0 × 24 = 0
Tan	3 × 20 = 60	1 × 24 = 24
Total	360	360

Draw a pie chart for the girls as shown on page 41 but using a protractor rather than a pie-chart measurer.

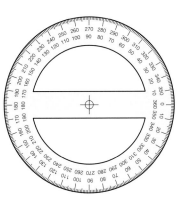

▶ A circular protractor is marked into 360 degrees, which is a complete turn.

Repeat steps one, two, and three for the boys. Since there are 15 boys, each one in the boys' column will have 24 degrees in this pie chart:

360 ÷ 15 = 24

The calculations are shown in the table at the top of this page, and the pie chart on the right.

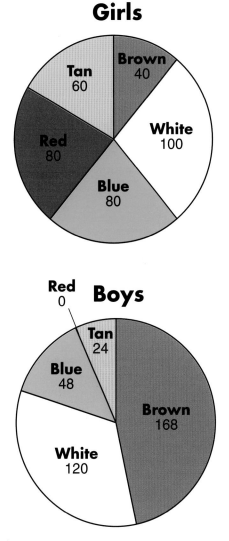

Girls

Boys

Comparing charts

The two pie charts show that a bigger <u>proportion</u> of the boys than of the girls was wearing white shoes, even though the same <u>number</u> of boys and girls were wearing white shoes.

What symbols mean

Here is a list of the common math symbols together with an example of how they are used. You will find this list in each of the *Math Matters!* books, so that you can turn to any book if you want to look up the meaning of a symbol.

— Between two numbers this symbol means "subtract" or "minus." In front of one number it means the number is negative. In Latin *minus* means "less."

= The symbol for equals. We say it "equals" or "makes." It comes from a Latin word meaning "level" because weighing scales are level when the amounts on each side are equal.

+ The symbol for adding. We say it "plus." In Latin *plus* means "more."

✗ The symbol for multiplying. We say it "multiplied by" or "times."

$$(8 + 9 - 3) \times \frac{2}{5} = 5.6$$

( ) Parentheses. You do everything inside the parentheses first. Parentheses always occur in pairs.

—, /, and **÷** Three symbols for dividing. We say it "divided by." A pair of numbers above and below a / or — make a fraction, so ⅖ or $\frac{2}{5}$ is the fraction two-fifths.

■ This is a decimal point. It is a dot written after the units when a number contains parts of a unit as well as whole numbers. This is the decimal number five point six or five and six-tenths.

Glossary

Other symbols used in this book.

≠ : The symbol for "is not equal to."

Terms commonly used in this book.

Average: A number that gives you, in different ways, a single typical value for the data you have. Most people use the word average when they are actually talking about the mean.

Carrying: In adding or multiplying, when the working column total is bigger than 10, this is the method of adding the left digit at the bottom of the column on the left.

Chart: A diagram used to show data from tables. There are many kinds of charts, including bar charts and pie charts. *See* Graph.

Column: Things placed one below the other. In a table the entries that are in a line that goes up and down the page.

Continuous scale: A number scale that increases smoothly.

Data: Information from which you start to solve a problem. You might have collected it yourself or have been given it. The word comes from Latin meaning "things given."

Digit: The numerals 1, 2, 3, 4, 5, 6, 7, 8, 9, or 0. Several may be used to stand for a larger number. They are called digits to make it clear that they are only part of a complete number. So we might say, "The second digit is 4," meaning the second numeral from the left. Or we might say, "That is a two-digit number," meaning that it has two numerals in it, tens and units.

Fraction: A special form of division using a numerator and denominator. The line between the two is called a dividing line.

Gate check: Four upright tally marks with a fifth drawn across them, looking like a gate. It is used to speed up tallying.

Graph: A diagram with two axes on which points are plotted and then joined by lines. *See* Chart.

Mode: One form of average. The number or the group of numbers that occurs most often in the data.

Percent: A number followed by the % symbol means the number is divided by 100. It is a way of writing a fraction.

Proportion: A comparative share in something.

Range: The difference between the largest and the smallest records in data. It tells you how widely the data are spread.

Row: Things placed side by side. In a table the entries that are in any line across the page.

Scale: A set of marks on a line used for measuring.

Sector: A piece of a circle, like a piece of a pie.

Separated numbers: Numbers that increase in jumps or steps. For example, shoe sizes increase through $6, 6\frac{1}{2}, 7, 7\frac{1}{2}$. You cannot get sizes between these numbers.

Spread: A number that tells you how variable data are. It is often measured using the range. *See* Range.

Symbol: A mark written on paper or something else to stand for a letter, a number, or an idea of any kind.

Table: An arrangement of rows and columns for sorting and storing data.

Tallying: Making marks as a way of recording the total.

Set index